KEEP YOUR EFFIN' DISTANCE

EAT FARTS

10 TEAR-O POSTCA

GREETINGS FROM EFFIN' BIRDS

Is this some kind of joke?

Pretty sure I'm dead and this is hell

Aaron Reynolds

GREETINGS FROM
EFFIN'
BIRDS

Aaron Reynolds

unbound

First published in 2021

Unbound
Level 1, Devonshire House, One Mayfair Place, London W1J 8AJ
www.unbound.com
All rights reserved

© Aaron Reynolds, 2021

The right of Aaron Reynolds to be identified as the author of this work has been asserted in accordance with Section 77 of the Copyright, Designs and Patents Act, 1988. No part of this publication may be copied, reproduced, stored in a retrieval system, or transmitted, in any form or by any means without the prior permission of the publisher, nor be otherwise circulated in any form of binding or cover other than that in which it is published and without a similar condition being imposed on the subsequent purchaser.

Internal and cover illustrations originally published in John James Audubon's *Birds of America* and Thomas Bewick's *A History of British Birds, Volume I* & *Volume II*

Text design by PDQ

A CIP record for this book is available from the British Library

ISBN 978-1-80018-058-1

Printed in Slovenia by DZS

1 3 5 7 9 8 6 4 2

A Note from the Author

Sometimes we just don't have the right words for a situation.

Maybe the emotions are too heavy and our words fail us, like at a wedding or a graduation or a funeral. There are specialty stores filled with nothing but cards for those scenarios.

But maybe we don't have the right words because we're dealing with an asshole. Some total piece of shit garbage person who makes our blood boil.

In that case, this book of tear-out postcards is for you.

Unbound is the world's first crowdfunding publisher, established in 2011.

We believe that wonderful things can happen when you clear a path for people who share a passion. That's why we've built a platform that brings together readers and authors to crowdfund books they believe in – and give fresh ideas that don't fit the traditional mould the chance they deserve.

This book is in your hands because readers made it possible. Everyone who pledged their support is listed below. Join them by visiting unbound.com and supporting a book today.

Barbara Aaron, Jennifer Abdo, Aurelian Adams, Georgia Adams, Hank Adams, Timothy Adams, Aethea, Amy Agler, Hailey Ahee, Paul Aho, Sascha Akhtar, Michelle Akin, Nicole Aldredge-Ward, Katy Alexander, Wee Ali, Magnús Þór Alísuson, April Alix, Diane Allan, Norma Alley, Rhona Allin, Constance Allison, amazingant, @anapupa_, Courtnay Anderson, Jordan Anderson, Rebecca Andrew, Dr. Nicole Angeli, Sophie Anggawi, Annetidepressant, Chrystal Antink, Cristina Aponte, Michael Aquino, Hugh Arai, Lauren Araki, Rhiannon Archer, Clare Arezina, Kristine Armstrong, Sapphira Armstrong, Steven Armstrong, Adrian Ashton, Nesher Asner, Julie Atwood, Toni Aurilio, Tom Avalon, Ruth Avelis, Roderick Axley, Bella Ayers, James Aylett, Dreamer Azri, Jess Bachaus, Laura Bailey, Lindsay Baker, Miri Baker, Chris Ball, Michael Balla Jr, Sarah E. Banks, Emily Barcelona, Sam Barclay, Andrea Barker, Tobin Barnecut,

Arminda Barnes, Austin Barnes, Molli Barnes, Raymond Barnes, Janet Barnette, Kathy Barron, Tanya Barrow, Robert Barten, Hannah Bartholomaus, Stacey Bartron, Jacob Bartynski, Jacob Bayless, Kate Beale, Felicia Becerra, Rae Becerra, Jill Beckman, Leah Beigler, Eric Bellmore, Gabe Bello, Joletta Belton, Kristi Benedict, C. Bennett, Julia Benson-Slaughter, Carmi Bentley, Richard Beres, Leighann Berg, Sharon Berg, Sara Berndt, Jillian Berninger, Deborah Bertsch, Simon Best, Andrew Bevan, Neal Bhatnagar, Tracey Birch, Christopher John Bird, Jeremy Bird, KC Bird, Merdif Birdif, Jeff Black, Pauline Blaimont, Noreen Blanluet, Rhonda Blasingame, Brett Blitzstein, Kelly Blount, Louise Boat, Karl Boehm, Patrick Bohan, Kevin Bohm, Megan Boing, Shirley Bomgaars, Erin Bontrager, Susan Booth, Adam Borden, Matt Bornski, Angela Boston, Theresa Bouchard Goddard, Carmen Bouchard Salvan, Katie Bouchillon, Clara Bouillet Lortet, Stacey Box, Patrick Boyd, Chris Bracken, Elizabeth Bradley, Jen Bradshaw, Sean Braisted, Josh Brand, Al Breda, Kathleen Brennan, Stephen Bridges, Susanne Broch, Willi Brooks, Mariah Brougher, Antony Brown, Owlizabeth Brown, Natalie Browne, Beka Bryer, Allison Buchanan, Kathleen Buchli, Stanley Buck, Jason Buell, John Bugay, Ryan Bunce, Nicole Bunting, Jason Buranen, Matthew Burger, Alan Burnham, Stephanie Kristen Burns, Joe Burt, Tai Buschert, Ben Bussey, Elizabeth Butcher, Jonathan Butler, Robin Butler, Sami Butler, Elizabeth Butterfield, Rebekah Byland, Daphne C., Kristal Caidoy, Tamara Caillouet, Briana Cain, Denise Caldwell, Sam Callaghan, Ryan Campbell, Patrick Cantwell, Adam Caplan, John Carden, Kate Carder, Ashley Cardona, Ellen Carlson, Dorothy Carman, Megan Carpenter, Laura Carscaddon, Barry Caruth, Jonathan Casali, Kate Casalino, Kristin Casper Bird, Emily Cassady, Davide Cattani, Daniel Cha, Debra Chaffins, Anne Chamberlain, Brad Chaney, Jamie Chapman, Rhian Chapman, Heather Chappelle, GJ 'Soup Can' Charlet III, Elizabeth Charlton,

Elizabeth Chase, Thaniel Chase, Kevin Chavis, Jillian Chilson-Pietruch, Serena Chryssikos and Craig Centro, Erica Ciupak, Caitlin Clark, Holli Clements, Angela Clifford, Maggie Cline De La Rosa, Laurel Coates, Laura Davis Cobin, Tyler Cochran, Katharine Coldiron, Jennifer Cole, Michael Coleman, Anne Collett, Ellie Collier, Clare Collins, Michael Collins, Joe Compeau, Megan Connolly, Joe Conway, Lauren A Cooper, Denise Cope, Annika J. Corley, Kim Corona, Gaby Corry-Mead, Janet Costello, Katy Costello, Rae Cote, Stuart Coulden, Elizabeth Cox, Jennifer Crackel, Thanh Cramer, Kristen Crandell, Kristen Crawford, Julie Creel, Sophia Croll, Bradley Crone, Alison Cross, Beth Crudele, Anthony W Crunk, Barbara Patrick Crunk, Kate Cruser, Carrie Cwiak, Jill Cypert, Ol d'Ybeaule, Jelena Dacres, Nick Dahl, Brian Dailey, Gabrielle Dainard, Kim Z. Dale, Nicole Daley, Mark Daniel, Jason Daugherty, Charlotte Davies, Sarah Davin, Carlton Davis, Molly Davis, Celeste Davis-Dill, Catherine Davis-Pauley, Megan Davy, Marleen De Becker, Gerdien de Galan, Johanna Blair de Haan, Veronica Deats, Brett Decker, Jim Dedman, David Dedrick, Jennifer Dedrick, Christopher DeFlumeri, Kara DeFrias, Tammy Deis, Mia del Barrio, Jessica DeMartini, Stevi Deter, Jennifer DeVenuti, John Dexter, Kelley Dhont, Alice Dibley, Sally Dick, Jen Dierker, Jason Diller, Marie Dillon, Libby Dixon, Katherine Dobbins, Thomas Docker, Rebecca Dodson, Eunice Dokko, Kimberly Dolphin, Heather Domin, Barry Dorrans, Claudette Dorsey, Carrie Dos Santos, Jennifer Douglas, Andrew Dowle, Claire Down, Cressida Downing, Susan Drake, Chloe Drane, Anne Druschitz, DTAC life, Mary Duffy, Michael Dugan, Julie Dumond, Michele Dunglinson, Rosanne Dunkelberger, Robin Dunlap, Lindsey Dunn, Matt Dunn, Heather Duquette, Ciro Durán, Estelle Dusk, Molly Dwyer, Nicole Dyszlewski, Amy Lynn Dzura, Roger Eads, Kathleen Eagle, Suzy East, Maria Easton, Katherine Eboch & Christopher L Jones,

Ariel Edwards, Olivia Edwards, Nicola Egert, Jax Elaina, Parker & Odie Ellena, Tara Elliott, Magen Ellis, Patricia Elzie-Tuttle, Pascale Engelmajer, Lacey England, John Erickson, Susan Erickson, L. Erskine, Phil Etting, Amanda Euen, Amy C. Evans, Kiersten Eyes, Corey Fake, Kathleen Farley, Megan Federline, Lisa Feistritzer, Richard Feldman, Adam Ferguson, Robert Ferguson, Molly Fergusson, Courtenay Ferris, Dr. A. Fiamengo, Carolyn Fiddler, Deirdre Fields, Kirk Fields, FiggyTree, Kath Finn, Jennie Fischer, Fiona E Fisher, Jade Fisher, Leah Fisher, Eileen Fitzpatrick, Jason Fitzpatrick, John Fitzpatrick, Catherine Flick, Ellen Flint, Barbara Florin, Sean Flynn, Tricia Fogarty, Anna Ford, Bradley Ford, Ruth Ford, Brent Foreman, Joseph Formoso, Natalia Forrest, Leslie Forrester, Charles Foster, Rhiana Foster, T Foster, Tammy Fotinos, Abby Fowler, Andrew Fox, Mary Fox, Rebecca Fox, Becky Frankenfield, Milane Frantz, Heather Frase, Sharon Freed, Angelica April Freeling, Linnea French, Cheryl Fretz, Megan Freund, Mary Beth Frezon, Julia Frickert, Cordella Friesen, Catherine Fritz, Courtney Fritzsche, Julia Frizzell, Curtis Frye, David Fryer, Barb Fulton, Tiffany Funk, C G, Suzanne L. Gabriel, Christopher Gaddy, Leah Galindo, Katie Gallivan, Kim Ganslein, Jacqui Garlick, Jordan Garrido, Jill Garza, Julia Gaunt-Rannala, Suzanne Gelwick Knight, Tamsin George, Marnie Gerkhardt, Hannah Geyik, Namir Gharaibeh, Courtney Gibbons, Andrea Gilbert, Gillelmus, Honor Gillies, Cyrena Gilpatrick, Sarah Glass, Judd Gledhill, John Gleissner, Abigail Goben, The Goddamned Delight Club, Samantha Godden-Chmielowicz, Tamar Godel, Goedzilla, Jennifer Goff, Allan Goldberg, Beth Goldfarb Jackson, Jessica Gonzalez, Jolie Good, Inga Gorslar, Brian Gosciminski, Mary Grab, Sarah Graber, Courtney Grant, Sarah Grant, Heather Gray, Tiffany Gray, Karen Greaves, Angie Green, Chris Green, Sonny Green, Thomas Green, Victoria Green, Carolyn Greener, Faye Greenslade, Keith Gregory,

Sabine Griebsch, Summer Griffis, Megan Griffiths, Bryan Grigsby, Barbra Grimmer, Amanda Griswold, Alex Groarke, Tiffany Groman, Lacy Grotheer, Emily Groveman, Victoria Grundle, Katy Guest, Alyssa Guido, Aaron Guilmette, Gillian Gunson, Cathy Gurson, Melanie Guthrie, Pamela Gutschalk, Brianne Haas, Alex Hacker, Carrie Hagan, Jeanne Haggard, Erin Haggerty, Susan Haigh, Carrie Hale, Kelly Hall, Michele Hall, Barry Hamilton, Matt Hamilton, Helen Hampson, Alyssa Hanna, Denise Hanson, Rachel Hanson, Andrea Hardesty, Jonathan Hardwick, Melissa Hardy, Margo "Ass Lady" Hardyman, Rebekka Harkins, Brian Harper, Kristina Harper, Kimberly Harrell, James Harrelson, Kate Harris, Elli Harris-Mevis, Kayla Hariss, Cadenza Harry-Heed, Amanda Hart, Sharon Hartley, Stephen Hartley, Keira Hartstein, David Haslem, Jenny Hawkyard, Molly Hayden, Maryanne Heard, Hedwig The Angriest Birb, Nicholas Hefling, Rebecca Heisler, hello haha narf, Matthew Hemler, Jan Hempel, Alison Hench-Saldana, Rachel Henderson, Jean Herbold, Matthew Herbold, Nikki Heron, David Hewlett, Mindy Hiley, Wilson Hill, Alison Hindenlang, Lisa Hobbs, Leah Hocking, Christopher Hockley, Kelly Hodapp, Sara Hoffman, Elizabeth Hogan, Suzanne Hogan, Carrie Holbo, Michelle & Craig Holigroski, James Hollingshead, Russell Hollins, Kate Holloway, Praemala Holt, Zac Holtz, Molly Honea, Brendan Hooley, Rachel Hoppins, Jessica Hopson, Andrea Horbinski, Lisa Horton, Rebecca Hotynski, Sarah Hotze, Kendall Houlihan, Claire Houston, Hrafnheim, Heather Huber, Robert Hubert, Joanna Hudson, Katy Huff, Andrea Hughey, Chris Hulbert, Bobbie Hullermann, Tyra Humphries, Kelly Hunter, Laura Hurley, Lee Hurst, Sony Huser, Jennifer Huskey, Kevin Hutchby, Greg Hyatt, Adair Iacono, Alexandra Iglina, Karen Ihms, Inkadinkadoo, a dedicated bird watcher, Margaret Ippolito, Hillary Irwin-Moran, Farah Ismail, Amanda Isom, Tagan Isted, Emily Ivie, Jennifer James, Maura James, Lucie Jammes, Pt Jarman,

Scott, Christina & James Jaworski, Wilma Jenkins, Jennifer, Jessica, Elaine Johnson, Jeanette Johnson, Mindy Johnson, Sophie Johnson, Vikki Johnson, Lynn Johnston, Sandi Johnston, Jennifer Jones, Kris Jones, Marina Jones, Martina Jones, Rebecca Jones, Tina Jones, Vicky Jones, Tobias 'knilch' Jordan, Karen Joy, Indra Joyce, jtheo, Jean Kalapathy, Ann Kamensky, Shannon Kampa, Helen Kanon, James Kaplan, Lisa Karahalios, Jeanne Karr, Shawnee Kasanke, Kate, Jeff Katin, KatyH, Kristine Kearney, Andrew Keck, Nick Keers, Kaitlyn Kelly, Mandy Kelly, MJ Kelly, Neal Kelly, Amanda Keltner, Robin Kemp, Maureen Kendzierski, Deirdre Kenny, Stephanie Keough, Mark Kerner, Zoe Kersey, Lori Kessler, Allison Ketchell, Miriam Ketonen, Courtney Keys, Bridget Kiely, Dan Kieran, Ania Kierczynska, Julie Kierstead, Carrie Kincaid, Carly King, Elana King, Dave Kinghan, Lisa Kingston, Christopher Kirby, Liz Kirby, Olga Kits, Darling Kittie, Catherine Klapperich, Ken Klavonic, Kerry Klewer, Erin Klodt, Madeline Knight-Dixon, Hannah Knox, Dawn Koch, Vernon Koch, Stacy Kolden, Laura Koot, S Korhonen, Laura Kramarsky, Katie Kreitzer, Kirschi Krempel, Christine Krikorian, Yulja Kryvoshei, Katie Kujala, Katie Kujawa, Sumitra Lahiri, Amelia Lahn, Laura Lajoie, Andrew R. Lake, Tiffany LaLonde, Sheila Lambert, Sarah Lambros, Connor Lambson, Jennifer Lamott, Jenny Lancaster, Sheila Lane, Robin Lange, Meredith Lapati, Phiip Lapin, Diana Laufenberg, Gina Lawrence, Gillian Lay, Renee Leader, Corey Leamy, Chris LeBlanc, Courtney LeBlanc, Aaron Lebovitz, Joanne Lee, Joyce Lee, Tucker Lee, Kathryn Lee Pope, Mike Lenker, Brandy Leonard, Nancy Lepano, Carolyn Leslie, Normandie Levas, Josh Levin, Robert Lewis, Natasha Leyk, Violeta Lialios-Bouwman, Jennifer Liechty, Jill Lightner, Georgia Lillie, Wey Wen Lim, Julie Linden, Sandra Lindquist, Jessica Linn, Jeff Little, Jonathan Litz, LJ, Robert Lloyd, Charlotte Lo, Andrew Local, Michele Lodin, Maggie Lofboom, Shirley Loh, Laura LoKKie, Pamela London, Sarah Long,

Amy Lord, Heather Lose, Patrick Lougheed, Erin Louttit, Kourtney Lowe, Beth Lowgren, Susan Lowry, Juliet Lu, Tom Lupfer, Elizabeth Lupton, Jese Lynn, Barney M, Uriah Mach, Siobhan Mackenzie, Edith Mackie, Timothy Madden, David Mader, Maget, Mino Mahdi, Daniela Mair, Bonnie Maize, Allison Malenfant, Lisa Maloney, Elliott Mannis, Tyrus Manuel, Abigail Marcus, Steven Margell, Dheeraj Maria, Maria, Lawren Maris, Judy Markowski, Maura Maros, Samantha Marshall, Brian Martin, Shellee Martin, Jessica Martinez, Tessa Marzulla, Jennifer Masciadrelli, Carrie Mason, Sarah Mason, Matthew Masten, Sarah Mathew, Eve Mathews, Shannon Matson, Sarah Anne Matthews, Jessica Mauerhan, Margot Maurer, maurezen, Grant Mauritzson, Jennifer Mauro, Lorien May, Jessica Mazloom, Jamie Mazzo, Robin McAleer, Amanda McCall, Scott McCall, Clifton McCarley, Yvonne Carol McCombie, Katherine McCord, Eric McCormick, Christy McCrady, Marianne McDonald, Rosie Mcdowell, Meghan McGaffin, Michael McGinn, Kathleen McGivney, Terri McGowan, Peta McGrath, David McGuigan, Jo McGuinness, Morgan McGuire, Carlizard McGurn, Michelle McHone, Steph McHugh, Kristen McIntyre, Cynthia McKenzie, Brandon McKinney, Jess McKnight, Patrick McKnight, Brian Mcleish, Tim McManus, Narn McMoo, Kathryn McNeil, Susan McNelis, Wendy McNiff, Anita McPherson, Megan McQueen, Travis McWaters, Debra Mead, Michelle Mead, Mary Means, Daniel Medina, Megan, Sage Mehew, Sarah Mei, Mein Lieblingsdepp <3, Chelsea Meister, Elizabeth Melton, Scott Mendenko, Andrea Mercado, Julie Mercer, R.L. Merrill, Emily Ann Meyer, Brittany Meyers, Genevieve Michaud, Michelle Michelbacher, Amelia Midkiff, Hannah Mieczkowski, Carra Milikien, MilkjugAlien, Betty Millard Stout, Cara Miller, Courtney Miller, Jill Miller, Monica Miller, Scott Miller, Shannon Miller, Trever Miller, Charlotte Milling, Steve J Minnix, Alison Minto, John Mitchinson, Jana Mlodzianowski,

James Moakes, Deena Mobbs, Larry Moeller, Jr., Milena Mois, Erica E. Molina, Amy Moller, Jamie Monachino, Christopher Money, Libby Mongue-Wymore, Dustin Moore, Matthew Moore, Heidi Moore Trasatti, Monica Moran, Carol Morency, Mark Morfett, Matthew Morgan, Caleigh Morr, Lori Morr, Kathy Morris, Emma Morrison, Jeannine Morton, Matteo Moschella, Caryl Mostacho, Katie Mountford, Katie Moussouris, Parjanya Mudunuri, Amanda Mullens, Robin Mulvihill, Julie A. Mund, Brandon Muramatsu, Stephanie Murdoch, Brenna Murphy, Maureen Murray, Richard Murray, Pinky Mx, Sandy Nairne, Maxine Najle, Adrienne Nakamura, Sue Nally, David A. Nance, Riki Napiorkowski, Jennifer Nardone, Vilmarie Narloch, Carlo Navato, Kelly Naylor, Tim Nelson, J.L. Nelson Kemp, Erin Nephin, Amanda Nerud, Erica Neubauer, Nancy New, Aaron Newton, Sarah Newton-Scott, Isabelle Nguyen, Joshua Nguyen, Eric Nickel, Harald Niesche, Amy Nighbor, Sam Nightingale, Kelley Nikondeha, Kari Nilsen, Luca Nixdorf, Kenya Nixon, Raziq Noorali, Sam Norbury, Vivian Norman, Kamille Nortman, Rene Norton, Talia Nudell, Nuschk, Meredith Nussbaum, Eric Nyman, Charles Peter Nystrom, Elspeth O'Donnell, Maeve O'Neil, Marcy O'Neill, Amanda O'Rourke, Ann O'Rourke, Keavy O'Shea, Barbara O'Brien, Lauren O'Brien, Vivian Obarski, Donna Oberhardt, Katrina Odom, Robin Ogata, Annie Ogren, Ursula OHara, Christopher Olive, Lori Olson, Al Orme, Yosie Ortiz, Rebecca Osborne, Allison Oseroff, Kaylyn Oshaben, William Otteman, Doug Otto, Melissa Otto, Melissa Owens, Sam Ozinga, Barb P., Eric Palicki, Tara Palmer, Rowshan Palmer Lang, Audra Pankiw, Erin Parrish, Erica Parson, Bryan Partner, Daphney Partridge, Nicki Patnaude, Dawn Patsel, Leslie Patt, Jeff Pattee, Samantha Pattenden, Adam Ross Patterson, Stevie Pattison-Dick, Beth Paul, Jonathan Paul, Krystal Payton, Noreen Pazderski, Lee M. Pearce, Erika Pearson, Maria Pearson, Leah Peasley, Kendra Pecan, Jen Peck, Meredith Peck,

Christina Pederson, Cara Peer, James Peifer, Allie Perry, Nicholas Perry, Vanessa Perry, Honor Peters, Margaret Peters, Bobbye Peterson, Colleen Peterson, Nichol Peterson-Kros, Karen Petronis, Christa Petryszyn, Abigail Phillips, Alison Phillips, Ella Phillips, Lawrie Fucking Phipps, Maïca Pichler, Bianca Pistoll, KerryLynn Pitt, Andreas Planck & Therése Haldin, Efimia Plantanitis, Jennie Pleasant, Marjorie No Fucks Given Pleiss, Åsa Plesner, Alison Plott, Valerie Polichar, Joanne Pollard, Justin Pollard, Katherine Polley, Amber Popovitz-Gale, Enmanuel Portes, Al Potts, Julie Powell, Tara Powell, Mary Anne Power, Laura Powers, Brian Pozun, Susan Pray, Mia Prensky, Cyndi Presnell, Elisa Price, Liam Price, Sarah Procunier, Shiraz Bird Provo, Sandra Prow, Angry Pug, Heather Purvin, Jacob Quail, Julie Quinsay, E. Ames R., Sofia R., Lucy Radford, Deborah Rahalski, Kristin Rainford, Michelle Ramos, Emily Ramsay, Melody Ramsbacher, Justin Randles, Hannah Rasing, Ayn Rassier, Matthias Raster, Paul Reavis, Beth Rechner, Judy Reed, Amelia Reep, Gus Reese, Kate Reeves, Meg Reeves, Jason Reigelsperger, Jamie Reighard, Amy Reilly, Elizabeth Reilly, Ken Reinertson, Casey Reit, Jeff Remer, Josie Remus, Jessica Repp, Lilly Reynolds, Joanna Rhind, Victor Ricchezza, Jessica Rice, Valerie Rice, Andrew Rich, Tara Richerson, Suze Rickard, Anna Ridley, Nancy Riegraf, Merel Rietveld, Bethan Roberts, CompletelyHatstand Roberts, Robin, Eric Robins, Heather Robinson, Kelly Robinson, Syd & Jeff Rock, Anna Roderick, Ahren Rogers, Angela Rogers, Eve Rogerson, Wojciech Rogoziński, Julia Rohs, David Rolf, Justin Romano, Jaime Romero, Nathalina Romeu, Christina Roosen, Nathan Ropelewski, Jennifer Rosen Heinz, Jessica Rosidivito, Faith Black Ross, Selena Ross, Peter Rossky, Vilhelm Rothe, Tara Rothwell, Anna Route, James Rowe, Jill Rowley, Chuck Ruether, Vickie Ruggiero, Brynmor Ruiz, Craine Runton, Christina Rupp, Michael Russell, Andrea Ryan, Eoin Ryan, Maggie S., Kelly Sabey, Anna Sadowski, Leslie Sadowski-Fugitt, Sara Sahlin,

Natalie Salhanick, Erin Salter, Mark Samuelson, Gael Sanchez, Julian Sanchez, Susan Sandenaw, Stephanie Sanders, Sarah Sanderson, Steph Sanderson, Aaron Sanstrum, Araceli Santos, Kris Sauter, Emma Savage, Renee Saviour, Sheryl Sawin, David Saxon, Jenna Scanlon, Diane Scarlet, Dylan Schadeck, Katherine Schaefer, Christopher Schappert, Donna Scheffki, Kaycee Schilt, Mirike Schmoß-Vidt, Tim Schorer, Dan Schulke, Carl Schultz, Connie Schultz, Maria Schwartz, Ace Schwarz, Anne-Marie Scott, Eric Scott, Lydia Scratch, Jean Scully, Robyn Seale, Kathryn Seaton, Jeremy Secaur, Doug Secrist, Kate Sedore, Martin Seehuus, Rivanna Segal, Lisa L. Seifert, Katherine Semel, SereneChaos, Gus Settle, Heather Sewell, Don Shadel, Tom Shakespeare, Jenna Shank, Kyle Shannon, Meg Sharkey, Leigh Sharp, Ashlea Shaw, Megan Sheehan, Kristin Sheldon, Theresa Shellen, Emily Shelton, Catherine Shen, Cristin Sheridan, Sherrill, Dmitry Sholokhov, Charlie Shrimplin, Eric Shwonek, Jamie Siglar, Christie Silkotch, Suzanne Simanaitis, Paige Simonson, Ehme Simpsano, Joseph Sireci, Kandis Sisson, Austen Sitko, Rob Sked, Mike Skelly, Slanestar, Anna Slater, Jessie Slater, Keith Sleight, Amanda Smith, Amy Smith, Emma Smith, Erin Smith, Hillary Smith, James Smith, Jo Smith, M Shernell Smith, Sophy Smith, Stacey Smith, Sue Smith, Elizabeth Smith-Fries, John Snethen, Kristine Snyder, David Sommer, Rain Soo Jamin, Fiona Soutar, Jonathan Sowers, Shannon Sparenga, Katharine Spencer, Jean Spinney, Ilona Spiro, Lucy Spoons & C-SPON, Wendy Staden, Hadley Stamp, Heather Stanavitch, Carmen Stang, Elizabeth Starkey, Desiree Statler, Kristyn Stauber, Naomi B. Steele, Dyon Stefanon, Emma Stefansky, Melissa Steinz, stellamnesiac, Kathryn Stelzer, Stephani, Kathryn Stephens, Kelly Stephens, Stacy Sterling, Sharon Stevens, Carilyn Stewart, Helen Stewart, Melissa Stewart, Dmitry Stillermann, Sandy Stith, Rebecca Stockbridge, Juliane Stockman, Sarah Stokes, Ruth Storey, Christopher Storm,

Nancy Stracener, JD Strong, Shannon Stypula, Victòria Subirana, Sam Sutor, Emma Sweet, Erik Swenson, Sarah T, Sharlea Taft, Shannon Taheny, Tim Talbert, Katrina Tanner, Emma Taylor, Georgette Taylor, Nate Taylor, Nicholas Taylor, Serena Taylor, Jeff Teather, Susie Tector, Judith Tegeler, Alison Teoh, Aaron & Rachel Terry, Kasi Tessmer, Ann Macaulay Thomas, Helena Thomas, Lauren Thomas, Paige Thomas, Ariel Thompson, Christine Thompson, Tyler Thompson, Holly Thorpe, Matthew Thyer, Heather Tibor, Carrie Tipton, Sara Titcomb, Patricia Tobar, D Tobias, Amie Tolomeo, Elizabeth Tompkins, Damia Torhagen, Galadriel Torres, Andrew Trainor, Baochau Tran, Michaeleen Trimarchi, Jane Trubridge, Joe Trollo, Melissa True, Lee Tucker, Joseph Turner, Lisanne Turner, Magdalena Twisselmann, Veronica Underhill, Jason Underwood, Tim Unrath, Rod Upton, Raymond Vagell, Shirin Vakil, Stephanie Van Riet, Rachael Van Riper, Kathy Van Ryzin, Kristi VandenBosch, Julie Vanderschaegen, Laura VanDruff, Nikki Vane, Suzan Vanneck, Debi Vans Evers, Brian Vasquez, Becky Vaughan, Deb Vaughn, Tara Veitch, Lorin Velikonja, Laurent Victorino, Sara Violante, Monica Virgilio, Jane Vivier, Laura Vrielynck, Shannon Wade, Waffles Friends Work, Stephanie Wagner, Julie Wallace, Deborah Walsh, Liz Walsh, Claire Wang, Jade Wanger, Carole-Ann Warburton, Angela Ward, Glenn C Warner, Maggie Warner, Alison Watkinson, Julie Watt, Rebecca Weast, Tom Weber, Julie Weber-Roark, Karen Webster, Wednesday and Willow, Martha Weekes, Rebecca Weibert, Evan Weinberg, Rachel Weiner, Melissa Weinstein, Hannah Wellman, Clint Weslager, Annie West, Ashley West, Gideon West, Jenny Westerman, Kristin Westphal, Cassandra Whalley, Amy Wheeler, Taylor White, Allison Whitehall, Teri Whitlock, Naomi Whittenbury, Carly Whyborn, Marzena Wicht, Wicked Good Playa, Katy Wight, Gillian Wilke, Margie and David Wilkins, Karyl Williams, Keri Williams, Mr Williams, Paul Williams, Catherine Williamson,

Katherine Willis, Leah Willoughby, Tammy Lynn Wills, Winged Pug Brew Labs, Wendy Winslow, Laura Winterstein, Coll Wise, Marcie Wise & Sam Freeman, Andrew Wiseman, Ann Withun, Cayla Witty, Adam Wolf, Rose Wolfson, Benedict Wong, Emily Wong, Alexandra Wood, Millicent Woodland, Laura Woods, Joni Wooldridge, Travis Workman, Rachael Worthington, Caroline Wrenn, Debbie Wright, Robert Wright, Siobhan Xavier, Xiofett, xlthlx, Amy Yoakum, Kerry Yoncak, Nicole York, Sarah York, Eli Young, Heather Young, Lori Young, Joanna Zattiero, Melina Zavala, Wendy Zebert, Gwenn Zeoli, Julie Zeraschi, Kathryn Zinman, Dan Zitelli, Jenn Zuko

I DON'T KNOW WHAT I EXPECTED BUT IT SURE AS FUCK WASN'T THIS SHIT

BIRD FACT: The dumbstruck ibis miraculously continues to have the capacity for surprise, even after all of the bullshit this past year has thrown at it.

THIS SUCKS AND I HATE IT

BIRD FACT: The dissatisfied warbler can almost always be found nesting in areas destined to make it unhappy.

WHY IN THE FUCK?

BIRD FACT: The snoopy hen asks questions to be seen asking them; answers are irrelevant and will frequently irritate it.

YOU ARE A GENUINE ASSHOLE

BIRD FACT: The candid shoveler uses "telling it like it is" as a cover for being a genuine asshole, and cannot understand why it is not invited to more parties.

WELCOME TO SHITSHOW CITY

BIRD FACT: The swill swallow nests in what could charitably be called a dump, and not just because it is full of garbage – the neighbours are also shit.

WHEN THIS SHIT IS ALL OVER, I AM GOING TO PUNCH YOU RIGHT IN THE DICK

BIRD FACT: The imperturbable oystercatcher surprises its prey with an unusual mix of patience and aggression.

ARE YOU DONE BEING AN ASSHOLE OR DO YOU NEED A FEW MORE MINUTES?

BIRD FACT: The longanimous cowbird has plenty of patience, just not for your bullshit. Take this as a sign you should fuck off immediately.

JESUS BUTT-HUMPING CHRIST

BIRD FACT: The transgressive longspur takes a particular delight in the discomfort of others and is skilled at obtaining a reaction with very few words.

THANK THE FUCKIN' LORD
FOR BOOZE

BIRD FACT: The pie-eyed phoebe's coping strategy for life involves self-medicating until all of its problems become fuzzy and indistinct.

WHAT DID I DO TO DESERVE THIS ENDLESS BULLSHIT?

BIRD FACT: Pique's chickadee can frequently be found writing letters to the editor and asking itself why it continues, decade after decade, to read this drivel.

SAVE YOUR EXCUSES FOR SOMEONE WHO GIVES A SHIT

BIRD FACT: The punctilious rail understands the fine distinction between caring and giving a fuck, and it uses that knowledge to survive in today's world.

TODAY IS MORE FUCKED UP THAN USUAL

BIRD FACT: The conspicuous diver is known for its ability to sense but not steer clear of danger. Scientists do not understand how the species avoids extinction.

MAYBE GET FUCKED OR SOMETHING?

BIRD FACT: The perceptive kite is not sure about much – except for the fact that you're a total piece of shit. It knows that for certain.

THE OPPOSITE OF
LIVE AND LEARN
IS DIE AN IDIOT

BIRD FACT: The dictum hobby speaks in fortune-cookie-esque aphorisms – except they're a whole lot meaner and don't come wrapped in delicious pastry.

OH WOW, A BUNCH OF DUMB MOTHERFUCKERS WITH DUMB MOTHERFUCKER OPINIONS

BIRD FACT: The miffed dove does not realise that we all know our management team are a bunch of fucking idiots and that we just bear it in silence.

SOMEONE SHOULD SHOVE BEES UP YOUR ASS

BIRD FACT: The bellicose hawk has a knack for taking every argument considerably further than polite society is comfortable with.

I'M GONNA GO LIVE IN THE MOTHER FUCKIN WOODS

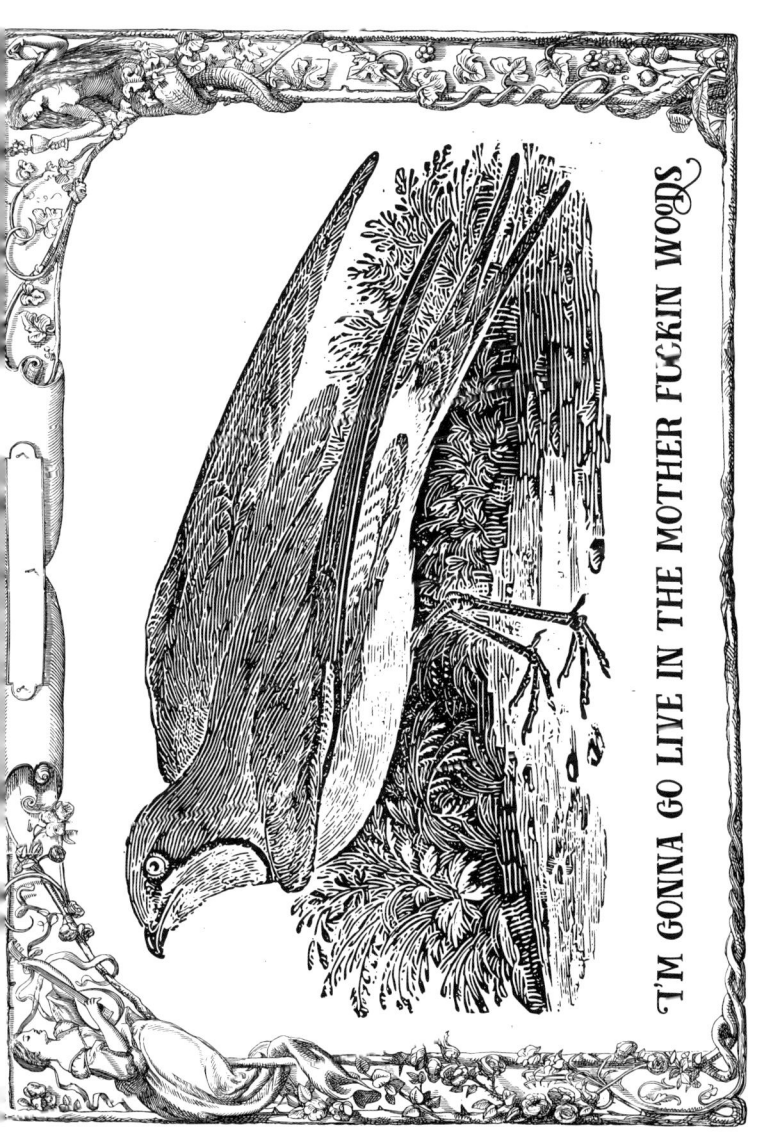

BIRD FACT: The hermit falcon deals with predators, irritating birds, adult decision-making and a litany of other daily frustrations by flying away.

THE TIME HAS FINALLY COME
FOR YOU TO FUCK YOURSELF

BIRD FACT: The stoic snipe can lie in wait for months or even years for a target to lower its guard before going in for the kill.

CAN WE TALK ABOUT HOW FUCKED THIS IS?

BIRD FACT: The bewildered gander can find something to be outraged about within two minutes of opening Twitter.

I AM GOING TO DEAL WITH THIS PROBLEM BY YELLING

BIRD FACT: Some will tell you that yelling is not appropriate when problem-solving. The vociferous gull will yell at those people for being fucking idiots.

EAT MY TURDS

BIRD FACT: The disgruntled coot, facing an adult future that looks like it's gonna suck, has reverted to playground insults as a coping mechanism.

HOLY MOTHER OF FUCK

BIRD FACT: The lukewarm osprey has moved past even pretending to care, and now barely goes through the motions of normal interaction at all.

GIVE ME A GODDAMNED MOTHERFUCKING BREAK

BIRD FACT: The weary sanderling suffers from a form of paralysis that prevents it from putting down its phone.

MOTHERFUCKER WHAT

BIRD FACT: The incredulous chickadee cannot believe what the fuck you are saying to it. Or at least that's what it keeps telling you. Why would it lie?

I'LL GIVE YOU TEN DOLLARS TO SHUT THE FUCK UP RIGHT NOW

BIRD FACT: The unburdened swift prefers to solve problems with money whenever possible.

SORRY THAT BEING A DECENT FUCKING HUMAN BEING IS SO INCONVENIENT FOR YOU

BIRD FACT: The needless petrel believes that empathy is for suckers, right up until the moment that it needs something from you.

WELL, IF IT ISN'T THE DUMBFUCKAROO GANG

BIRD FACT: The adjudicating kingbird can always be relied upon to deliver a devastating assessment of whoever just walked into the room.

YOU KEEP TALKING WHEN YOU SHOULD DEFINITELY SHUT THE FUCK UP INSTEAD

BIRD FACT: The indifferent drake is absolutely able to hear you; it just does not give a shit about what you have to say.

FUCK ALL THIS

BIRD FACT: The vamoose goose knows that if the going gets tough, you should have fucked off way earlier, and it expects you to learn from this mistake.

WHAT FUCKING DAY OF THE WEEK IS IT?

BIRD FACT: The bridled oriole is one stumble away from total collapse. Right now is fine; thirty seconds from now is maybe okay. Ten minutes? Who knows.

ALL I ASK IS FOR ONE BULLSHIT-FREE DAY

BIRD FACT: The swamp pigeon prays that each new day will be different, despite all the evidence that it will be exactly the same as every other day.

FUCK YOU, I'M ANGRY

BIRD FACT: Unlike some birds that can see a wide range of colours, the splenetic eagle can only see red.

YOU CANNOT IMAGINE HOW MUCH
I FUCKING HATE THIS IDEA

BIRD FACT: The cogent owl has a reasonable explanation for why it hates your idea, though if pressed, it will admit that it's because it's yours.

WE'RE MAXED OUT ON CLUSTERFUCKS OVER HERE

BIRD FACT: The knackered dipper is at the mercy of the news cycle, no matter how much effort it makes to disconnect.

TELL ME MORE ABOUT THAT TIME YOU FUCKED OFF

BIRD FACT: The forthright heron is generally a bird one wants as an ally, though it can be devastating to sit across from one during an annual review.

PRETTY SURE I'M DEAD AND THIS IS HELL

BIRD FACT: The resigned junco has finally figured out the functional difference between hell on earth and actual hell: absolutely nothing.

GLAD TO SEE YOU ARE STILL A FUCKING IDIOT

BIRD FACT: Gauge's bittern would be shocked to discover that things have improved but also refuses to take any responsibility for the lack of improvement.

MAYBE LET'S NOT DO THE STUPIDEST FUCKING THING WE CAN THINK OF

BIRD FACT: The censorious crane has strong opinions about all things, especially every decision you've made in your entire life.

WHY WOULD WE LISTEN TO AN EXPERT INSTEAD OF A DUMB MOTHERFUCKER WHO TALKS REALLY LOUD?

BIRD FACT: The pundit dunlin eschews expertise in favour of folksy wisdom or common sense, even when reality shows up to kick its ass.

SOME ASSHOLES DO NOT DESERVE YOUR ATTENTION

BIRD FACT: The rock-ribbed bluebird has learned that responding to cries of 'debate me' in their Twitter mentions yields no positive results at all.

IT MUST BE A GREAT COMFORT THAT NOTHING IN YOUR LIFE HAS EVER BEEN YOUR FAULT

BIRD FACT: The adroit phainopepla's expectation that everyone else in its workplace is reasonably smart and capable is sadly misplaced.

KEEP YOUR FUCKIN' DISTANCE

BIRD FACT: The cognisant catbird will violently repel other birds that enter into its personal space, especially if they're not wearing masks.

I AM SO FUCKING TIRED ALL THE TIME

BIRD FACT: The depleted harlequin has been neglecting self-care for so long that it does not remember what a good night's sleep feels like.

ACCORDING TO YOUR
HOROSCOPE, FUCKING OFF
IS IN YOUR FUTURE

BIRD FACT: The prophetic pintail knows that you will fuck off eventually, but it plans to do everything it can to move up your fucking-off timetable.

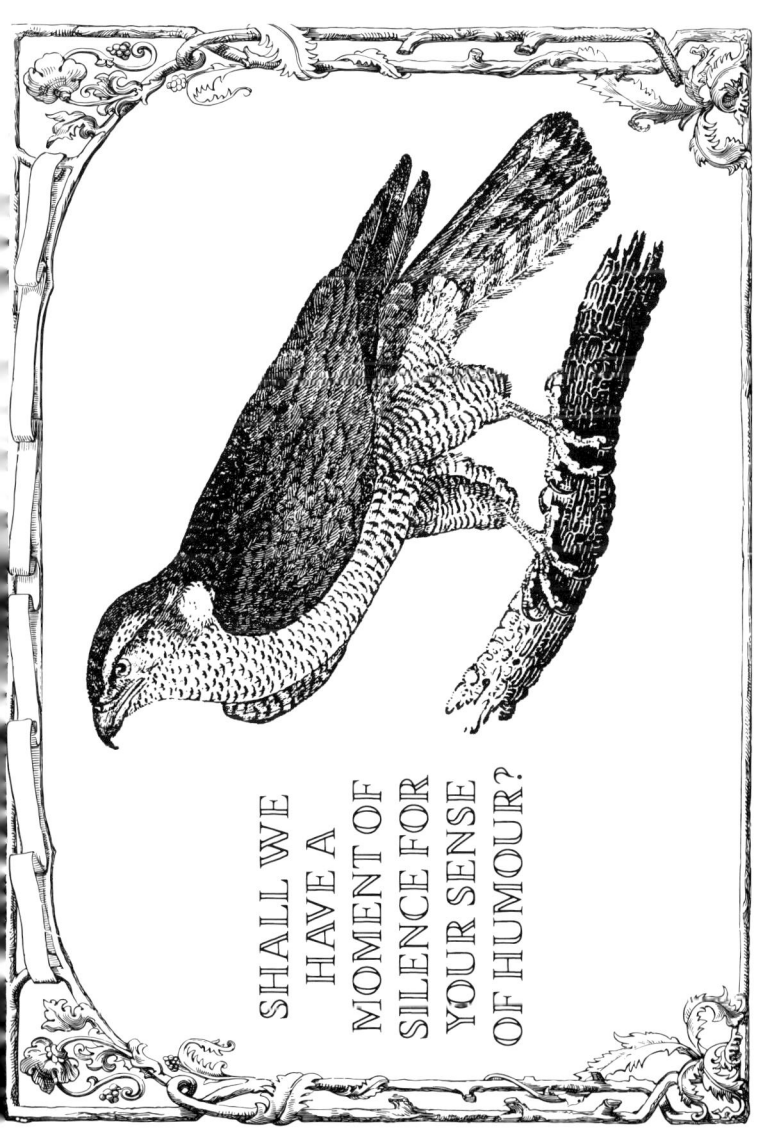

SHALL WE HAVE A MOMENT OF SILENCE FOR YOUR SENSE OF HUMOUR?

BIRD FACT: If you challenge a heinous goshawk to explain why its joke is funny, it will call you a rude name and leave.

OF COURSE I'M ANGRY,
YOU DUMB PILE OF FUCKS

BIRD FACT: The oblivious kinglet is finely attuned to the moods of the characters on its favourite show but blind to those of the people around it.

WHAT IN THE ALMIGHTY FUCK?

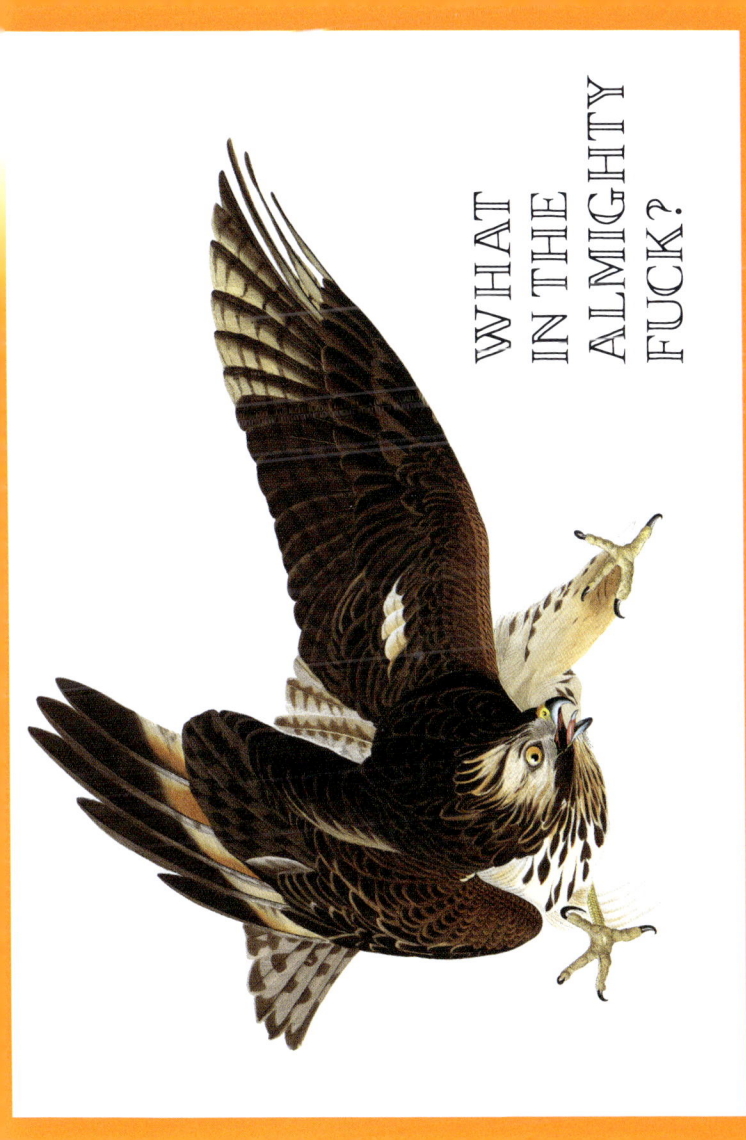

BIRD FACT: Every time the stupefied shearwater thinks it has witnessed the most fucked-up thing it has ever seen, it turns out to be wrong.

CAN WE HAVE A BREAK BETWEEN CLUSTERFUCKS?

BIRD FACT: The stupor auk experiences the world through a mind-blown haze. Notable features: glassy eyes, vacant responses, frequent naps.

IS THIS SOME KIND OF FUCKING JOKE?

BIRD FACT: The morose wigeon has no time for shenanigans, malarkey, tomfoolery or really anything that could be classified as fun.

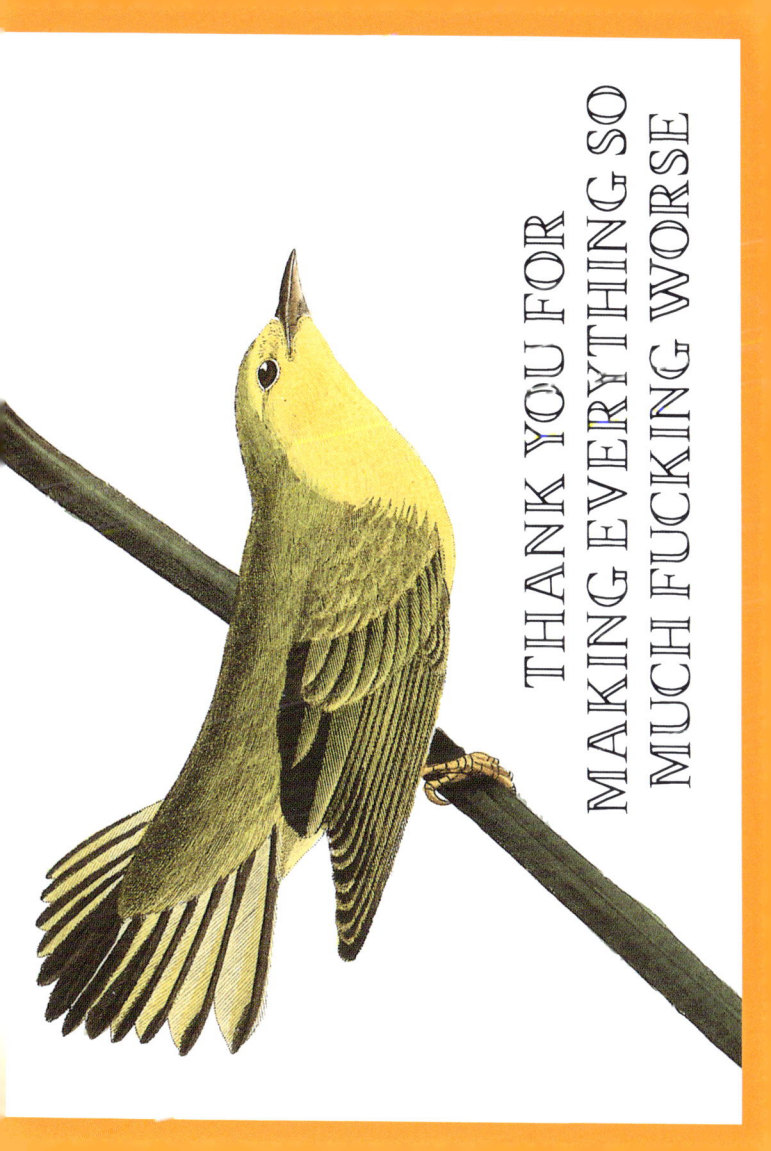

THANK YOU FOR MAKING EVERYTHING SO MUCH FUCKING WORSE

BIRD FACT: The snide curlew does not know what you mean when you suggest that it is being sarcastic. It insists that it would never consider such a thing.

OH JOY, ANOTHER DIPSHIT WHO THINKS HE UNDERSTANDS MY AREA OF EXPERTISE

BIRD FACT: The competent cormorant fights a constant battle against other birds that think because they have a confident, loud voice, they are also experts.

SHOVE OFF, DICKBUCKET

BIRD FACT: A discourteous bunting can both shock with its coarse yet precise language and amaze with what you are pretty sure are made-up words.

DID YOU GET SOME KIND OF VOLUME DISCOUNT ON STUPID FUCKING OPINIONS?

BIRD FACT: The pontifical warbler knows the difference between a fact and an opinion but does not let that get in the way of dunking on celebrities on Twitter.

OH, FOR FUCK'S SAKE

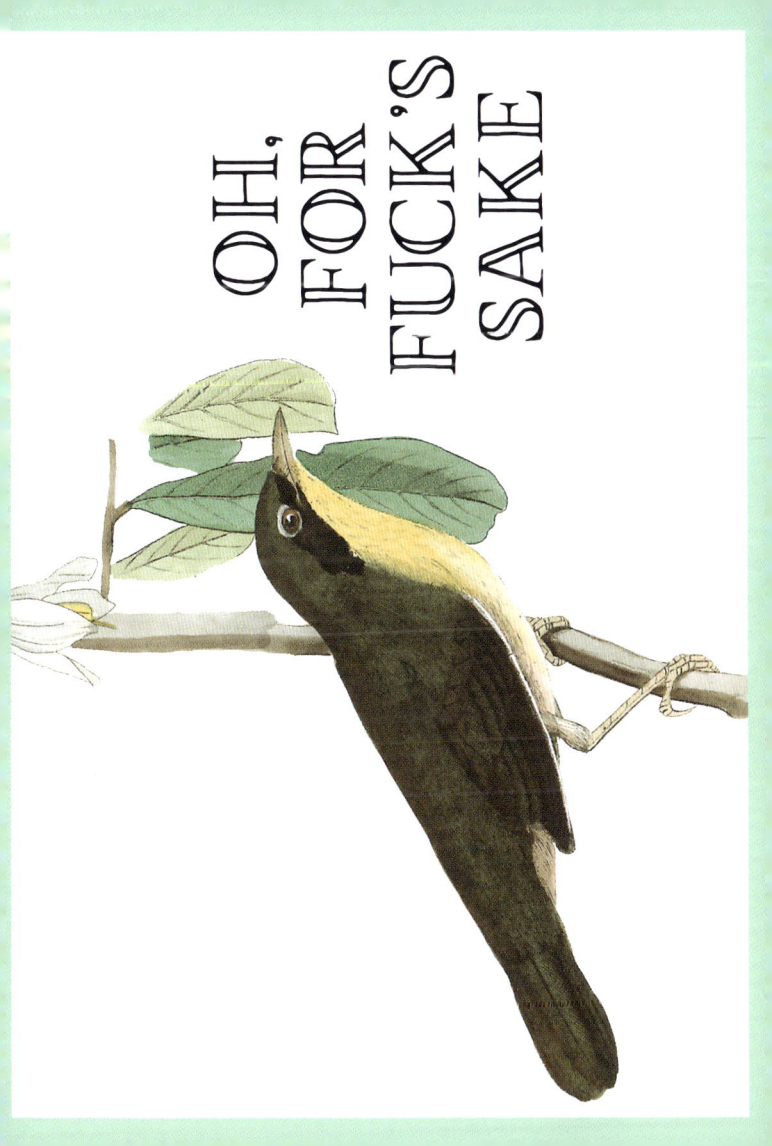

BIRD FACT: The prognostic albatross knew this bullshit was coming but could not avoid it, prompting it to ask what the fuck foresight is good for.

FEEL
FREE
TO EAT
SOME
SHIT

BIRD FACT: The indulgent grackle can sound like it is giving you a compliment when it is definitively not.

I AM UNSURE AS TO WHY I SHOULD GIVE A FUCK ABOUT YOUR OPINION

BIRD FACT: The trifling quail is not sure why it bothered to hear you out, since it was certainly never going to give a shit about what you were saying.

WELL, LAH-DE-FUCKIN-DAH

BIRD FACT: The disregarding creeper does not give a single fuck about your bullshit and will happily let you know, over and over again, until you fuck off.

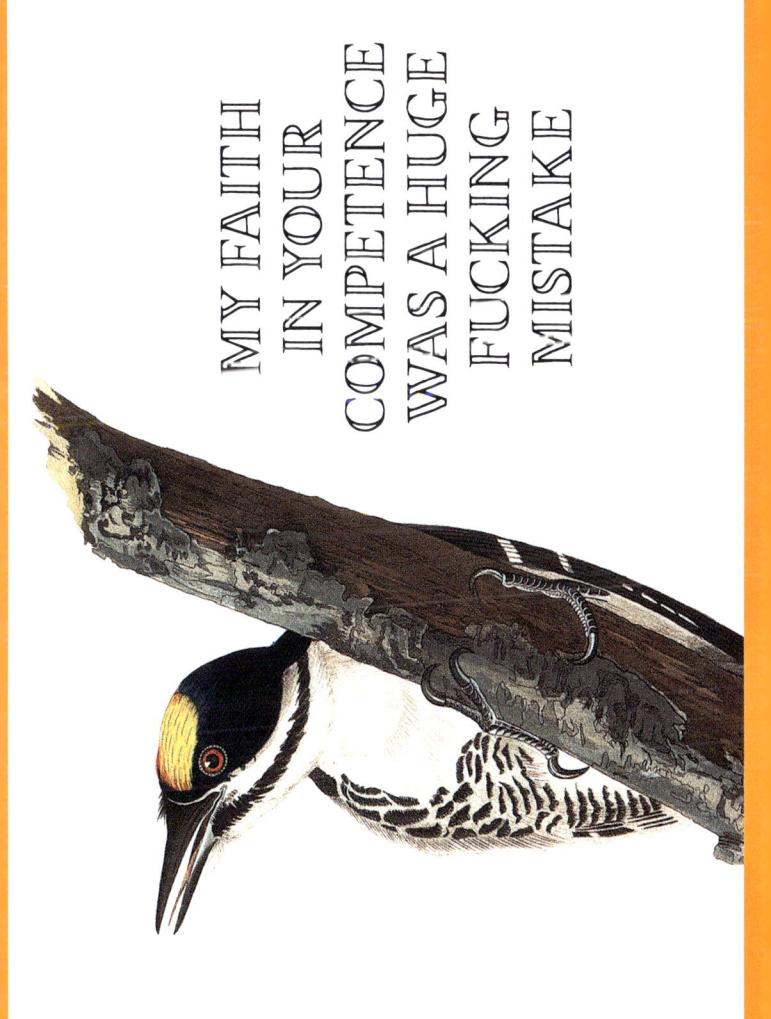

MY FAITH IN YOUR COMPETENCE WAS A HUGE FUCKING MISTAKE

BIRD FACT: The gloomy sapsucker pretends to have an optimistic outlook, but as soon as things turn bad, it cannot wait to revel in disaster.

TODAY IS NOT THE DAY TO FUCK WITH ME

BIRD FACT: If there were such a thing as a fuckometer, you would not be mistaken to visualise the aggrieved wren's as pegged at zero.

EXCUSE ME WHILE
I GET THE FUCK
OUT OF HERE

BIRD FACT: Skeddadle's crow knows exactly when to get the fuck out of a situation. If you spot one nearby, keep your eye on it and follow its lead.

I AM JUST FUCKING DONE

BIRD FACT: The swamped gnatcatcher would very much appreciate a reset button for all this bullshit. Sooner rather than later, please and thank you.

IS IT 'BRING A DUMB-ASS MOTHERFUCKER TO WORK' DAY?

BIRD FACT: The uppity redstart has been unable to cope with the idiocy of its co-workers for something like a decade now.

I'M READY TO FUCK UP SOMEONE'S SHIT

BIRD FACT: The seething pipit can switch from a pleasant companion to a fierce adversary, ready to burn everything to the ground, in moments.

GOD FUCKING DAMMIT

BIRD FACT: The flustered grosbeak doesn't know which of these straws broke the camel's back, but Christ on a bus, there are a lot of motherfucking straws.

HOLY FUCK, MY BRAIN IS TIRED

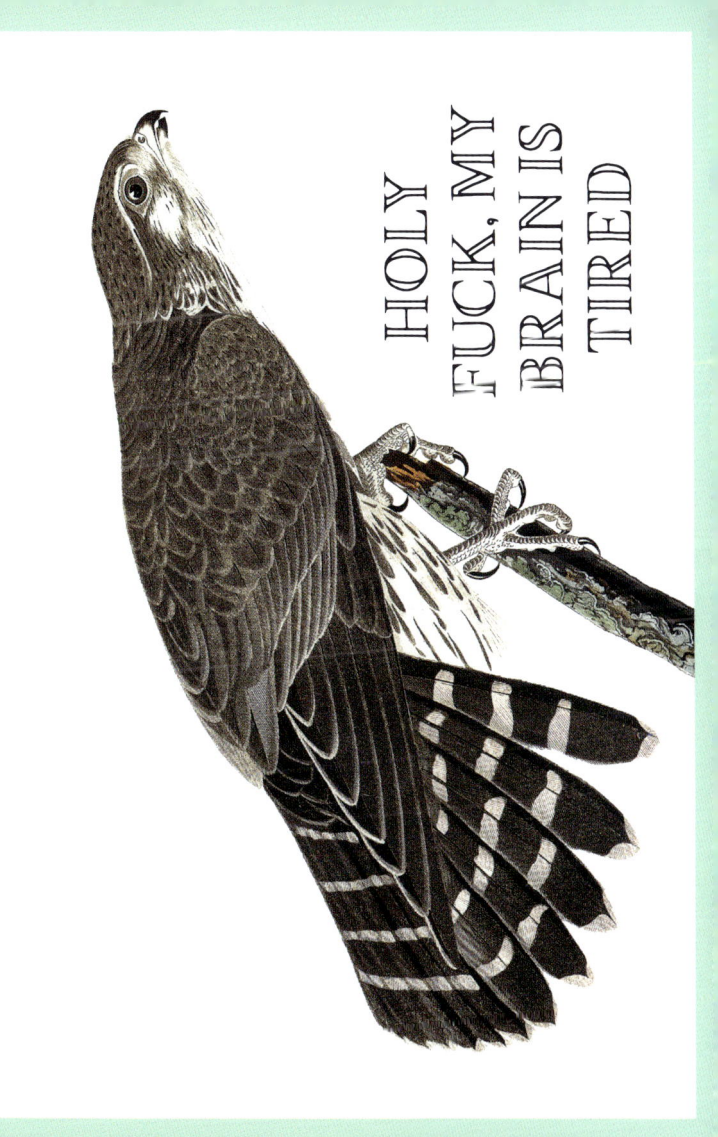

BIRD FACT: The frazzled godwit knows that it has reached its bullshit tolerance, but somehow it feels compelled to come back for more.

WHAT THE FUCK?

BIRD FACT: The quashed spoonbill has realised the futility of its outrage and is not going to expend any more emotional bandwidth on all this bullshit.

TALKING TO YOU WAS A HUGE FUCKING MISTAKE

BIRD FACT: The contrite sparrow does not try to dodge its responsibility: it knew you were an asshole before it started talking to you.

I HAVE FEELINGS

BIRD FACT: The woebegone eagle would like everyone else to just fuck off for a while and leave it alone, okay?

I HATE PEOPLE

BIRD FACT: If you make eye contact with a reclusive titmouse and it immediately looks back down at its phone, it DOES NOT WANT TO TALK TO YOU. Take the hint and move the fuck on.

I HAD A BEAUTIFUL DREAM WHERE YOU WERE ALL COMPETENT AT YOUR FUCKING JOBS

BIRD FACT: The dime-store raptor pays the minimum but expects the maximum and can't quite reconcile that with its disappointment in employee results.

JESUS FUCK, YOU DUMBSHIT

BIRD FACT: The exasperated kingbird understands why it needs co-workers, but it still daydreams endlessly about the day when robots can replace idiots.

IT HAS COME TO
MY ATTENTION
THAT YOU ARE A
HUGE FUCKING
DICKWEED

BIRD FACT: The condemnatory sandpiper has seen all this shit before and will see all this shit again. It feels no remorse about calling out this shit as shit.

SHUT YOUR FUCKIN' MOUTH BEFORE I SHIT IN IT

BIRD FACT: The paramount shrike takes everything too far but then blames the blowback on everyone else being overly sensitive.

PEOPLE ARE THE FUCKING WORST

BIRD FACT: It is impossible to see an eremite swan without travelling to the deserted wasteland where it lives. It is equally difficult to get one on the phone.

THIS WENT FROM ZERO TO CLUSTERFUCK IN A HURRY

BIRD FACT: The Cassandra tern saw all this shit coming, and yet it did nothing to prevent it aside from repeatedly saying, 'Can you believe this shit?'

HOW LONG IS THIS BULLSHIT GOING TO TAKE?

BIRD FACT: The fretful scaup is on its last remaining thimbleful of patience and would like you to hurry the fuck up and do whatever you're going to do.

THANKS FOR SHOWING THE REST OF US WHAT A TRASH FUCKER YOU ARE

BIRD FACT: The immoderate crossbill is actually thrilled that you revealed yourself to be a total piece of shit. Now it can stop wondering about it.

FUCK THIS SHIT, LET'S GET DRUNK

BIRD FACT: The acquiescent loon figures that if the world is gonna burn, it's gonna burn, and there's no value in living through the end of civilisation sober.

NO ONE HERE ORDERED A FUCKIN' FIASCO

BIRD FACT: The disaster dowitcher's cry sounds remarkably like, 'Clusterfuck! Clusterfuck! Clusterfuck!'

WHAT THE FUCK, KAREN

BIRD FACT: The egocentric pochard's natural habitat is the line at Starbucks, screaming at the barista about the temperature of the almond milk.

NEXT TIME YOU FEEL LIKE BEING A PIECE OF SHIT, JUST STAY HOME

BIRD FACT: The melancholy goosander drags all the other birds down with it through a combination of complaining, eye-rolling and dramatic sighs.

COULD YOU SHOVE YOUR QUESTION UP YOUR ASS?

BIRD FACT: The inelastic plover has heard enough bad-faith 'just asking' questions to last a fucking lifetime, thank you very much.

THERE IS NO SCENARIO IN WHICH I WANT MORE OF THIS SHIT

BIRD FACT: The decisive murrelet knows precisely how much shit it can handle and has become skilled at setting limits so it does not lose its mind.

DID THE COMMON SENSE FAIRY LEAVE
A DOLLAR UNDER YOUR PILLOW?

BIRD FACT: The erudite meadowlark understands that not everyone is a genius, but it marvels at how many people are utter fucking nincompoops.

HOLY SHIT, I HATE ALL OF THIS

BIRD FACT: The conversant grackle has become suddenly, achingly aware of the shortcomings of its life.

WHY AM I WATCHING THIS FUCKIN' GARBAGE PARADE?

BIRD FACT: The passive eider knows that its brain is gonna rot if it keeps watching this shit, but it just cannot help itself.

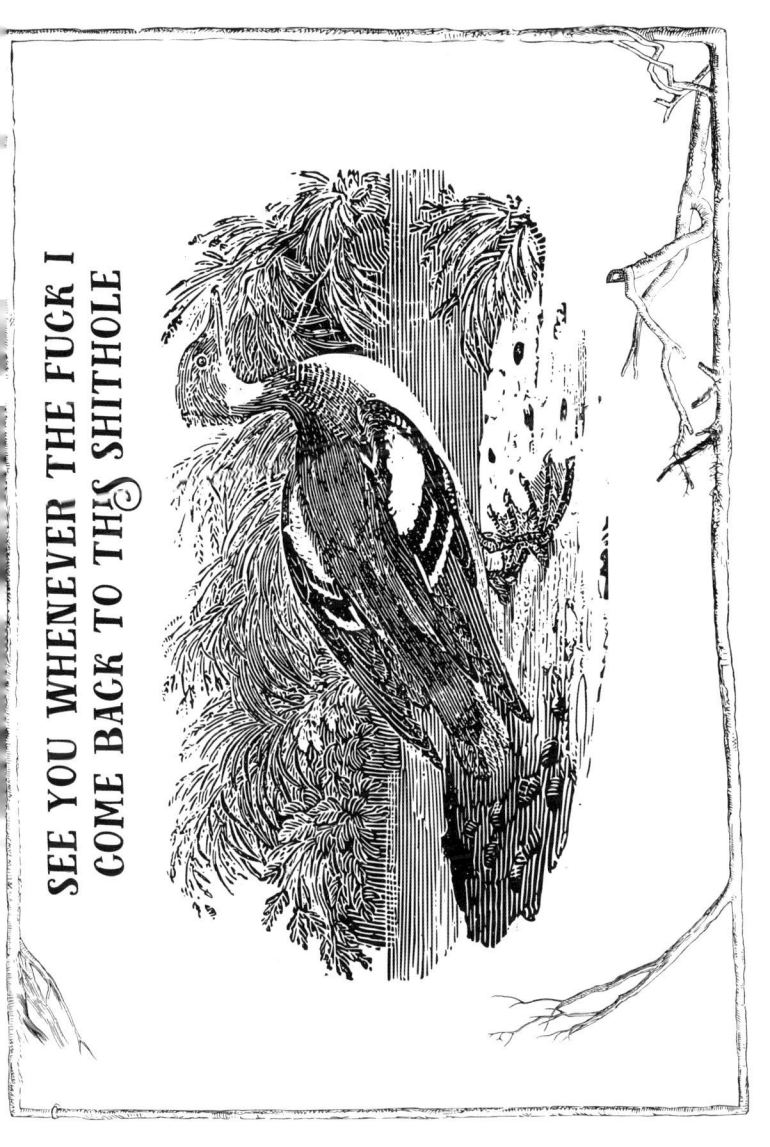

SEE YOU WHENEVER THE FUCK I COME BACK TO THIS SHITHOLE

BIRD FACT: People often wonder where the absent parula has gone, not realising that it left to get away from them.

JESUS FUCK AND A HALF

BIRD FACT: The affronted tanager knows what is about to happen but will stick around anyway for the opportunity to loudly proclaim how offended it is.

DON'T BE A PIECE OF SHIT

BIRD FACT: The injunctive ovenbird sees the path you're headed down and would like to caution you against transforming into a full-on fuckwit.

YOUR PRIORITIES ARE FUCKED

BIRD FACT: The assessing vulture knows that you make the wrong choices. It has a hard time figuring out its own shit but won't let that stop its trash-talking.

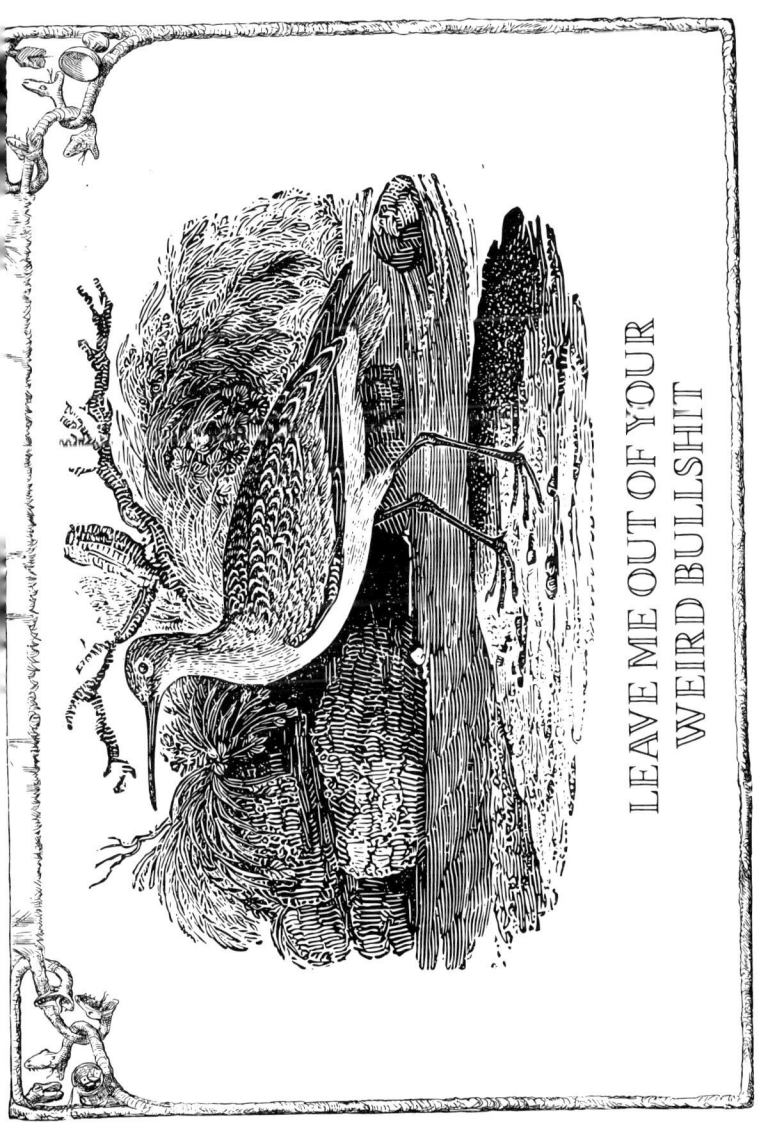

LEAVE ME OUT OF YOUR WEIRD BULLSHIT

BIRD FACT: The aloof merganser does, in fact, understand your weird bullshit – and that's exactly why it wants to be left out of it.

I'M DIZZY FROM HOW MUCH I'M ROLLING MY FUCKING EYES

BIRD FACT: The consummate scoter developed a taste for the finer things early in life and now cannot be bothered with anything less than the best.

HAVE YOU CONSIDERED NOT BEING A SHITHEAD?

BIRD FACT: The constructive mockingbird thinks that it is making helpful suggestions, but it is not.

I AM LOSING MY FUCKING MIND OVER HERE

BIRD FACT: The rational sheldrake is certain that things were normal once and at some point stopped being normal – but that timeline is fucked.

WHADDUP WIENERS

BIRD FACT: The ostentatious osprey has this nagging feeling that it is irritating everyone around it, but it doesn't know what to change or even if it wants to.

THAT'S SOME GANDALF-LEVEL WIZARD SHIT RIGHT THERE

BIRD FACT: It is very difficult to know if the scoffing finch likes or hates you, because it delivers every piece of praise and derision in exactly the same mocking tone.

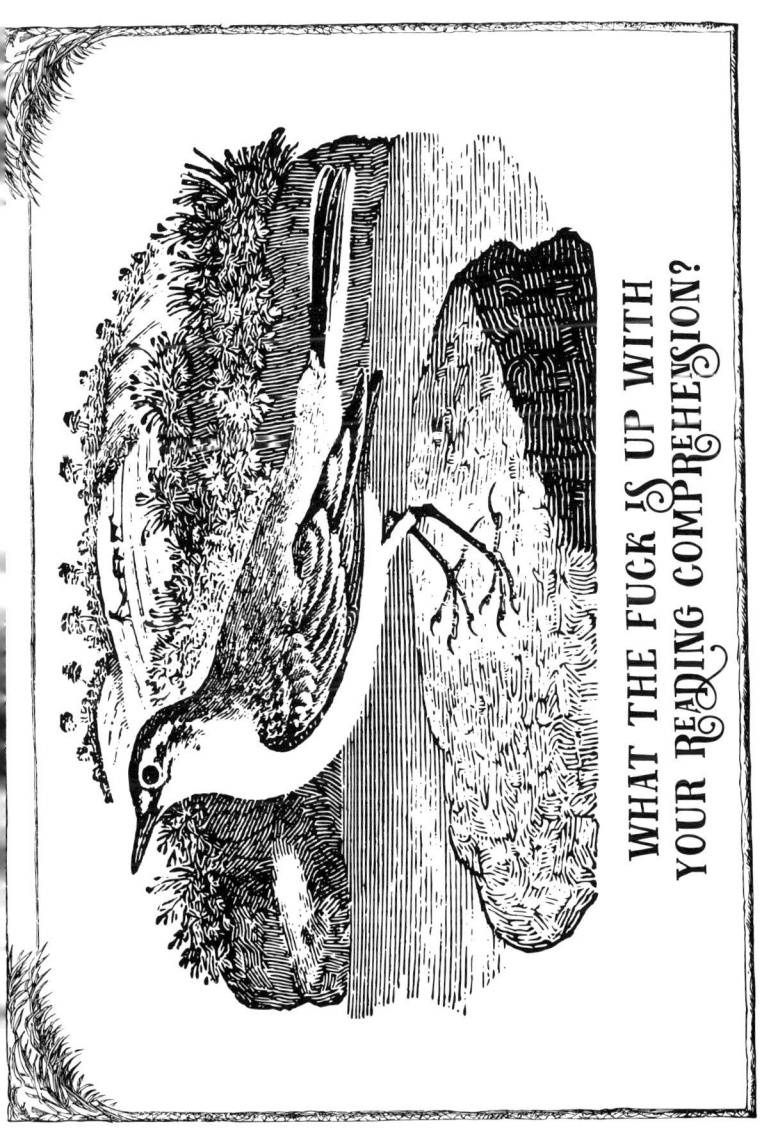

WHAT THE FUCK IS UP WITH YOUR READING COMPREHENSION?

BIRD FACT: The assessing steamer duck will pick at a perceived failing of your social media post, not realising that they misread it and are making an ass of themselves.

CAN TODAY'S BULLSHIT AT LEAST BE DIFFERENT FROM YESTERDAY'S BULLSHIT?

BIRD FACT: The narked gull's life would be considerably easier if it took advantage of the fact that it can fly away whenever it likes.

THE SEASONS MAY CHANGE, BUT YOU WILL ALWAYS BE AN ASSHOLE

BIRD FACT: The acquiescent longbill finally understands that some people plain old suck ass and there's nothing that can be done to change them.

FUCK ALL THIS, GOODBYE

BIRD FACT: The furred egret is not here for your gatekeeping takes on what is or is not considered a bird. Keep that shit to yourself.